First published in Great Britain 2022 by Farshore
An imprint of HarperCollins*Publishers*
1 London Bridge Street, London SE1 9GF
www.farshore.co.uk

HarperCollins*Publishers*
1st Floor, Watermarque Building, Ringsend Road Dublin 4, Ireland

Written by Claire Philip
Images used under license from Shutterstock.com

© The Trustees of the Natural History Museum, London 2022

ISBN 978 0 0085 0769 5
Printed in Romania
001

Parental guidance is advised for all craft and colouring activities.
Always ask an adult to help when using glue, paint and scissors.
Wear protective clothing and cover surfaces to avoid staining.

A CIP catalogue record for this title is available from the British Library.

MIX
Paper from
responsible sources
FSC® C007454
FSC
www.fsc.org

NATURAL HISTORY MUSEUM

DINOSAURS

ANNUAL 2023

CONTENTS

OUR PLANET 8
TRICERATOPS 10
MAZE CHALLENGE 12
SPINOSAURUS 14
DINOSAUR DISCOVERY 16
INVESTIGATING THE PAST 18
BRACHIOSAURUS 20
DINOSAUR DOODLES 22
COLOUR BY NUMBERS 23
APATOSAURUS 24
SPOT THE DIFFERENCE 26
DINOSAUR EXTINCTION 28
PTERANODON 30
DINO LEAF COLLAGE 32
PACHYCEPHALOSAURUS 34
ONLY JOKING 36
GEOLOGISTS 38
PARASAUROLOPHUS 40
CRETACEOUS CARD CRAFT 42
CORYTHOSAURUS 44
COLOUR BY NUMBERS 46
JOIN THE DOTS 47
PREDATOR VS PREY 48
GIGANOTOSAURUS 50
DINOSAUR DISCOVERY 52
ARCHELON 54
CODE BREAKER 56
FOSSILISED FOOTPRINTS 57
TODAY'S DINOSAURS 58
TROODON 60
WORD SEARCH 62
CROSSWORD 63
COELOPHYSIS 64
WHO AM I ? 66
TRUE OR FALSE? 68
ANSWERS 69

NATURAL HISTORY MUSEUM

Packed full of fun facts and awesome activities!

DINOSAURS
ANNUAL 2023

This book belongs to

....

....

Write your name here

Turn the page to turn back time. Get ready to meet the dinosaurs!

OUR PLANET

Life on Earth has changed a lot since it began. Lots of animals have come and gone – and humans are quite new!

Earth's History

Our planet's history has been divided into periods of time called eras. These eras are further divided into periods that begin and end with significant events, such as mass extinctions. The timescale below charts the evolution of life on Earth.

| 900 | 480 | 410 | 310 | 245 | 66 | 50 | 0.3 | Millions of years ago |

The first insects develop

Reptiles first emerge

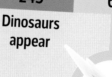

Dinosaurs die out

Humans evolve

First multicellular life forms appear

Bony fish evolve

Dinosaurs appear

Mammals expand greatly

8

Glossary box:

When multiple species die out more quickly than they can evolve, there is a mass extinction event.

The Age of the Dinosaurs

The Mesozoic era was made up of the Triassic, the Jurassic and the Cretaceous periods. It was during this time, between 245 and 66 million years ago, that all kinds of dinosaurs roamed the Earth, along with many other creatures such as other reptiles, fish and insects.

Triassic Period
252–201 million years ago

Around 252 million years ago, the Triassic period began after an enormous extinction event that changed the Earth forever. The early dinosaurs emerged as almost all of Earth's previous species died out.

Jurassic Period
201–145 million years ago

The Jurassic period followed the Triassic. During this time, plants such as ferns and horsetails flourished, which gave herds of giant plant-eating dinosaurs plenty to eat.

Cretaceous Period
145–66 million years ago

During the Cretaceous period, dinosaurs diversified – meaning many more species developed. Huge meat-eaters such as T. rex hunted their prey, and heavily armoured plant-eaters grazed widely.

Small Coelophysis was one of the early dinos.

Super-sized Diplodocus lived in the Jurassic period.

T. rex roamed Earth during the late Cretaceous era.

 GRUNT!

TRICERATOPS
One of the toughest dinos of all time!

Three horns used in self-defence

Beak-like mouth

Jaws lined with hundreds of teeth

Nice Frills!

Triceratops had a large, bony frill around its neck that could grow up to 1m (3ft) in height. Experts believe this body feature was used to attract mates or to help the dinosaurs spot each other!

DINO FACTS

Name: *Triceratops*

Meaning: *"Three-horned face"*

Size comparison:

Food: *Plants*

Danger rating: *4/10*

Habitat: *Forests and plains where there were plenty of plants*

 BASH!

Late in the Game

With its large, stocky body and three large horns, the easily recognisable Triceratops stomped across North America in small family groups. It lived around 70 million years ago – quite close to the end of the dinosaur period.

Large, bony frill protected its neck

Living Together

There is fossil evidence to suggest that young Triceratops banded together in small groups as they grew up. This would have given them added protection from deadly predators – there is safety in numbers.

Strong Teeth

Even though Triceratops looks like it could have been a super tough hunter, it only ate plants. Its extra strong teeth allowed it to chew through all kinds of vegetation, including the thickest shrubs. Tasty!

Simple Dino-doku

Complete the grid by drawing the correct dinosaur in the empty spaces. Make sure there is only one of each dinosaur in each column and each row.

Answers on page 69.

MAZE CHALLENGE

This geologist can't find his way to the field site! Can you help him find his way back – and collect the tools on the way?

Watch out for dead ends!

START

FINISH

Answers on page 69.

13

SPINOSAURUS

This enormous meat-eater snapped up large fish from ancient rivers.

Watch Out!

Weighing up to 8 tons – that's more than 5 cars – this fish-eating giant was even bigger than the mighty T. rex, one of the most well-known carnivores of all time!

SWOOSH!

SPLASH!

Long, narrow snout like a crocodile

DINO FACTS

Name: *Spinosaurus*

Meaning: *"Thorn lizard"*

Size comparison:

Food: *Meat*

Danger rating: *8/10*

Habitat: *Swamps and tidal flats*

In the Water

It is thought that Spinosaurus could swim and that it spent much of its time in water. This would have allowed it to get up close to its fishy prey.

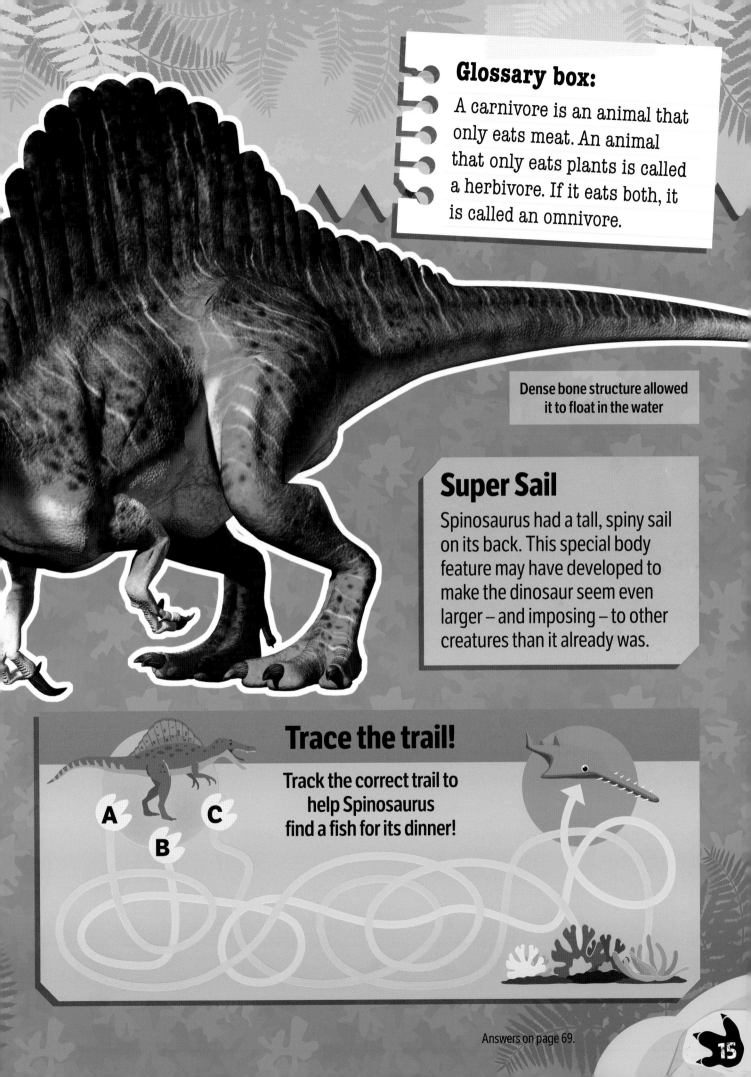

Glossary box:

A carnivore is an animal that only eats meat. An animal that only eats plants is called a herbivore. If it eats both, it is called an omnivore.

Dense bone structure allowed it to float in the water

Super Sail

Spinosaurus had a tall, spiny sail on its back. This special body feature may have developed to make the dinosaur seem even larger – and imposing – to other creatures than it already was.

Trace the trail!

Track the correct trail to help Spinosaurus find a fish for its dinner!

A   B   C

Answers on page 69.

DINOSAUR DISCOVERY

Let's go on an expedition to find some dinosaurs.
How many of each dino can you spot below?

Write your answers here.

Answers on page 69.

INVESTIGATING THE PAST

How do scientists make new dinosaur discoveries?

Fossil Clues

Paleontologists are scientists that study life on Earth by searching for and examining fossils.

Fossils are the preserved remains of animals and plants found in rock. Every so often, new dinosaur fossils are found and brand new species are discovered!

From Bone to Fossil

For a fossil to form, the animal needs to die somewhere that it can be easily preserved, for example in water. As the flesh rots away, only the hard skeleton remains. Gradually, the skeleton is covered by layers of sand and mud. Over millions of years, this transforms the bone into a rock-like substance — a fossil!

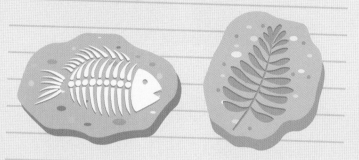

Searching for Clues

To find dinosaur fossils, paleontologists travel to sites where it is known that there is rock from the Triassic, Jurassic or Cretaceous periods. They use maps that show special features, such as the height of the land, then start scanning the area on foot.

BRACHIOSAURUS

The giraffe-like dinosaur that snacked on trees!

DINO FACTS

Name: *Brachiosaurus*

Meaning: *"Arm lizard"*

Size comparison:

Food: *Plants*

Danger rating: *3/10*

Habitat: *Flat plains*

Nibble, Nibble!

Brachiosaurus' very long neck and tall front legs (which were longer than its back legs) allowed it to reach leaves on high-up conifer trees. It also munched through ferns, cycads, horsetails and other ancient plants.

Legs like pillars

Very long tail

Small head on long neck

Chisel-like teeth

Nose to Tail

Brachiosaurus measured between 25–30m (85–100ft) in length – that's as long as a blue whale! If you were to stand beside it, Brachiosaurus would have towered above you at an impressive 9m (30ft) in height. That's as high as two double-decker buses!

MUNCH!

CHOMP!

Big Family

This enormous creature belonged to the sauropod dinosaur group, along with the

well-known dinosaur Diplodocus and Apatosaurus (see page 24). All of these long-necked giants thrived during the Jurassic period and were the largest land animals to have ever walked on Earth.

Which Comes Next?

Can you order these dinos from smallest to largest number of spots?

A

B

C

D

E

Answers on page 69.

DINOSAUR DOODLES

It's drawing time!
Read the instructions to finish off this ancient forest scene.

Draw your favourite meat-eating dinosaur at the front of the picture.

Add clouds to the sky.

Add a plant-eating dinosaur in the background.

Add an erupting volcano in the background.

Add some ancient plants, such as ferns or conifer trees.

Draw a boulder.

22

COLOUR BY NUMBERS

This Styracosaurus needs colouring in!
Use the colour key to complete this dinosaur picture.

23

APATOSAURUS

One of the most famous sauropods!

Long tail gave the dino balance

Stocky, tree trunk-like legs

DINO FACTS

Name: *Apatosaurus*

Meaning: *"Deceptive lizard"*

Size comparison:

Food: *Plants*

Danger rating: *4/10*

Habitat: *Swampy riverbanks*

Small to Big!

This huge dinosaur laid eggs the size of basketballs! When the babies hatched, they were about 30cm (1ft) long, but as adults they measured 23m (just over 75ft). Now that's what I call a growth spurt!

CHOMP!

GULP!

Tiny head

Great Grazer

Apatosaurus mostly grazed on low-lying grasses and plants such as ferns, eating 400kg (almost 900lb) of plant matter every single day. It may have also used its long neck to reach up high for leaves.

Chew Your Food

This long-bodied dinosaur didn't chew its food. Instead, it swallowed large stones to help it crush and digest the many plants it munched. These stones are known as gastroliths. Some animals alive today use them too, such as crocodiles and alligators.

Dino Dots Join the dots to finish the picture, then colour it in!

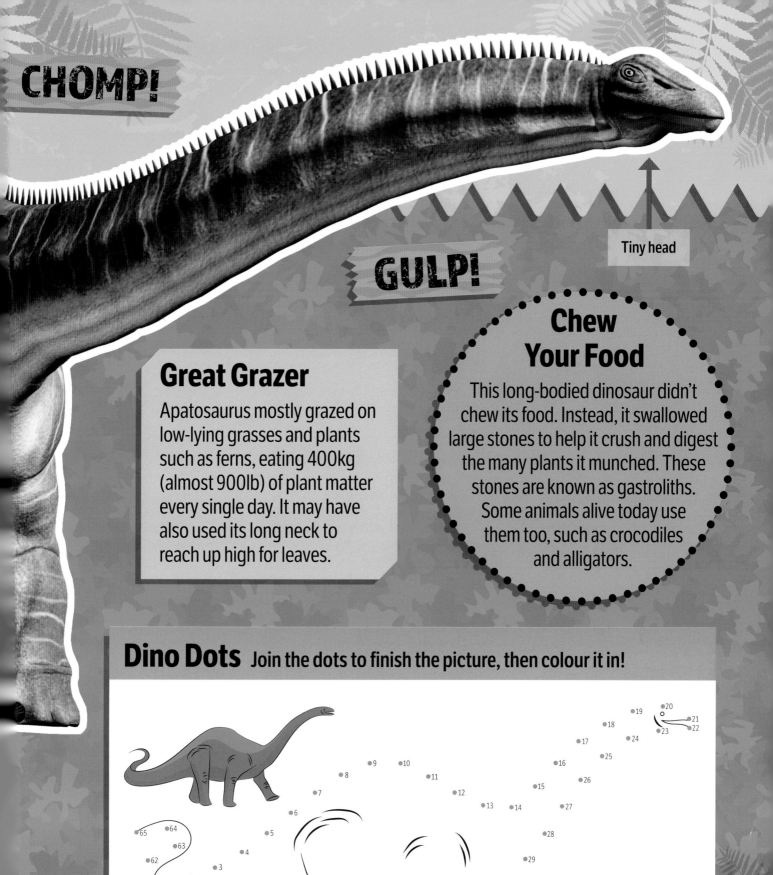

SPOT THE DIFFERENCE

How quickly can you spot the eight differences between the two pictures?

Set a timer and see how long it takes you to find them all!

Ask a friend to have a go – who was the quickest?

It took me ☐ minutes and ☐ seconds to find all the differences.

Circle each difference you find. Colour in the leaves as you go.

DINOSAUR EXTINCTION

What happened 66 million years ago?

Extinction Event

The dinosaurs lived successfully for many millions of years until something happened that caused them to die out completely. Like many other species before them, they were affected by a mass extinction event.

While we don't know for sure, many experts believe that a giant asteroid may have hit Earth, creating conditions that made the planet uninhabitable for the dinos.

Mega-Volcanoes

Something else was happening on Earth at this time, too. Supervolcanoes, far bigger than any that exist today, were erupting – a lot. These massive volcanoes are thought to have spilled unimaginable amounts of lava, causing havoc with the dinosaur's habitat. They may have been caused by a gigantic earthquake triggered by an asteroid.

Getting Hotter

Fossil records show that there was a huge increase of carbon dioxide in the Earth's atmosphere 66 million years ago. Perhaps the asteroid smashed into rock that held the gas and released it? The huge increase in carbon dioxide raised the planet's temperature, which had a huge impact on life on Earth.

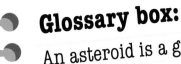

Glossary box:

An asteroid is a giant space rock that travels around the Sun.

The Big Chill

Soon after the asteroid hit, there was large-scale cooling of the planet. Dust and gas thrown up into the sky would have blocked out heat and light from the Sun. This would have made the climate far colder, making survival difficult.

One Quarter Left

It is thought that 75% of all species were wiped out, including many marine animals. Others, such as crocodiles and birds, did survive. In the aftermath of the extinction event, new species emerged – including lots of mammals and eventually humans.

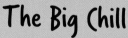

PTERANODON

A highly aggressive flying reptile!

DINO FACTS

Name: *Pteranodon*

Meaning: *Pteron means "wing"
and anodon means "toothless"*

Size comparison:

Food: *Fish*

Danger rating: *7/10*

Habitat: *Near the sea*

Body Size

Pteranodon's height when standing would have been about the same as a tall adult human – around 1.8m (6ft). When it opened its wings to their full width, they reached an impressive 5.5–7m (18–23ft). Now imagine standing eye-to-eye with that!

Dinner Time!

It is believed that Pteranodon flew in large groups over open water in the hunt for tasty fish to eat. Fossilised fish bones and scales have been found with Pteranodon remains.

Dino Neighbour

Pteranodon was one of the biggest of the pterosaurs – a group of flying reptiles that were distantly related to, but not actually, dinosaurs. They lived during the Triassic era until the end of the Cretaceous period, dying out with the dinosaurs.

Mysterious Crest

This flying creature's notable head crest may have developed over time to attract mates – or it may have helped it balance during flight. Its body structure was streamlined and built for soaring speeds.

SNAP!

Hollow bones to help it fly

No teeth – but an extremely sharp beak like a bird

Small body compared to its large wingspan

Spot the Dino! Which of these close-ups shows a Pteranodon?

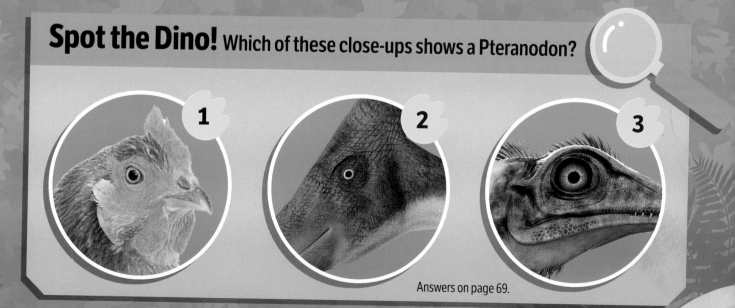

1

2

3

Answers on page 69.

DINO LEAF COLLAGE

Let's get crafty with some natural materials!
Collect some leaves to create some roar-some dino pictures.

You will need:

- Leaves of various colours and sizes
- Newspaper to protect your surface
- PVA Glue
- Paper or card
- Googly eyes, pens or paints

Instructions:

1 Use our examples as a guide or get creative and make your own dinosaur!

2 Cover your surface with newspaper before you begin.

3 Layer and arrange the leaves on your piece of paper or card until you are happy with your collage, then glue in place.

4 You can use googly eyes or draw eyes using a pen or paints.

Ask an adult to help ⚠️

ROAR!

T. REX

PTERODACTYL

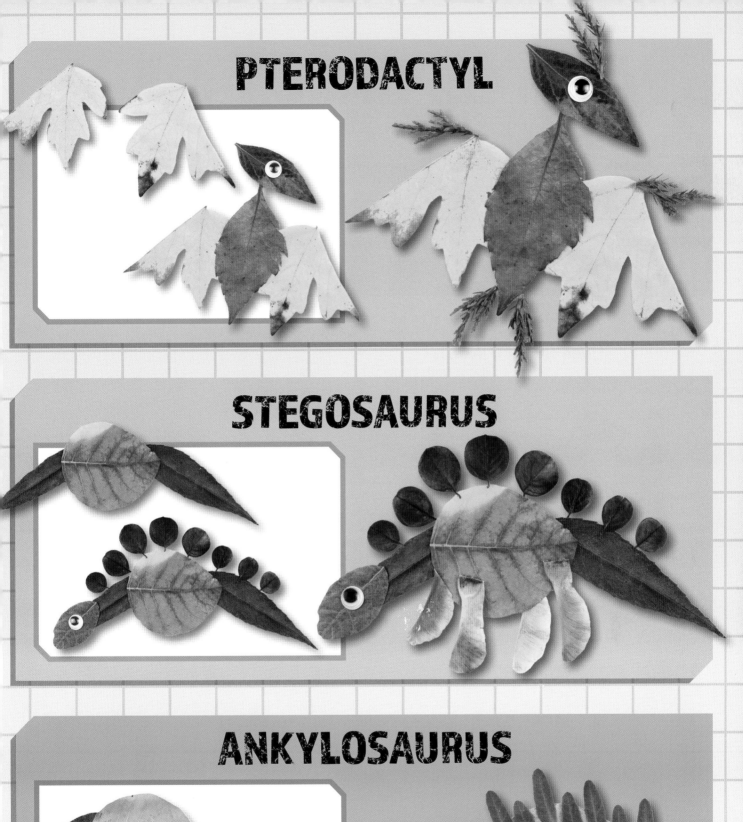

STEGOSAURUS

ANKYLOSAURUS

PACHYCEPHALOSAURUS

This thick-skulled dinosaur may have fought by headbutting its opponents!

DINO FACTS

Name: *Pachycephalosaurus*

Meaning: *"Thick-headed lizard"*

Size comparison:

Food: *Plants*

Danger rating: *5/10*

Habitat: *Woodland, meadows and grasslands*

Bashing Heads!

Pachycephalosaurus is easily recognised by its thick skull plate, which may have been used during battles between males or possibly even to attract mates. It was 25cm (10in) thick!

Spiked nose

Thick, domed skull

Tiny Bites

Its small teeth weren't that tough, which suggests that Pachycephalosaurus may have eaten a diet of bite-size leaves, fruit and possibly insects, too.

BASH!

Odd One Out

Which of these dinosaurs is different from the rest?

1

2

3

Answers on page 69.

CRACK!

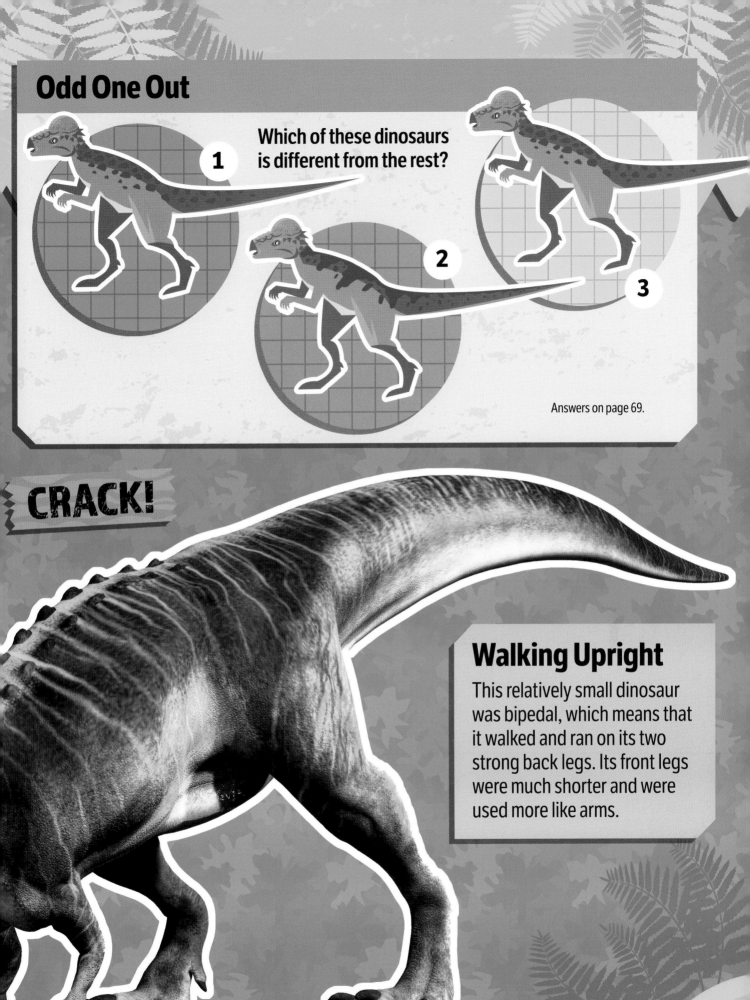

Walking Upright

This relatively small dinosaur was bipedal, which means that it walked and ran on its two strong back legs. Its front legs were much shorter and were used more like arms.

ONLY JOKING!

Can you match the answers to these pre-hysteric dino jokes?
Try them on a friend!

Question 1
What do you call a boring dinosaur?

Question 2
How do you ask a T. rex if it would like a hot drink?

Question 3
What's on the roof of a dinosaur's house?

Question 4
Which type of dinosaur would make a good police officer?

Question 5
Why did the geologist give up their career?

Question 6
What do you call a bunch of singing Edmontosaurus?

Question 7
What do you get if you cross a dinosaur with a lime?

Question 8
What do you call a dinosaur that hates losing games?

Ha! Ha!

Answer A
A really 'saur-loser!

Answer B
It was too rocky!

Answer C
A dino-sour!

Answer D
Tricera-cops!

Answer E
Rep-tiles!

Answer F
A Dino-snore!

Answer G
An Edmonto-chorus!

Answer H
Tea, Rex?

Answers on page 69.

GEOLOGISTS

A geologist is a scientist that studies the history of our planet
— they are detectives of the Earth!

What is Geology?

Geology is the branch of science that deals with the study of Earth and all its different layers, as well as the natural materials that make them up!

Rocks and Minerals

Much of our planet is made up of rocks and minerals that formed deep within the Earth. Geologists study these rocks because they can give us clues to the past. The three main kinds are called igneous, sedimentary and metamorphic.

Igneous
Granite

Sedimentary
Limestone

Metamorphic
Slate

Layer by Layer

The earth is made up of five different layers, as seen in the picture here. Geologists record and examine the effect of shockwaves (caused by earthquakes) as they travel through the different layers, to learn more about them.

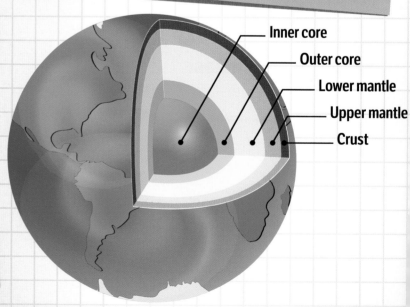

Inner core

Outer core

Lower mantle

Upper mantle

Crust

In the Field

Geologists go on expeditions called field trips to collect rock samples. They use special tools such as handpicks and rock hammers to collect pieces of rock, which they take to special labs for further investigation.

Could you be a Geologist?

Do you have what it takes to become a geologist?
Take this short quiz to find out!

Do you like being outdoors?	**YES / NO**
Do you like investigating the past?	**YES / NO**
Are you interested in how life on Earth has evolved?	**YES / NO**
Do you think rocks are cool?	**YES / NO**
Would you like to predict earthquakes?	**YES / NO**

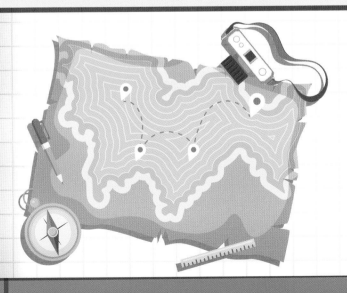

If you answered **YES** to the questions above, you may have found the job for you!

39

PARASAUROLOPHUS

This duck-billed dinosaur made loud trumpet sounds!

Hadrosaur Family

At 5m (16ft) tall, Parasaurolophus was one of the largest members of the hadrosaur dinosaur group, which lived during the Cretaceous period. Hadrosaurs, also called duck-billed dinosaurs, are identified by their head crests and wide, beaked mouths.

DINO FACTS

Name: **PARASAUROLOPHUS**

Meaning: **"Argentina lizard"**

Size comparison:

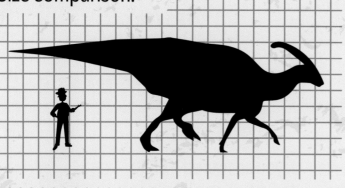

Food: **Plants**

Danger rating: **3/10**

Habitat: **Forests, plains and swamps**

Safety in Numbers

These hadrosaurs lived in large herds, which gave them protection from dinosaurs such as Albertosaurus – a big meat-eater that lived at the same time. If they felt threatened, they may have sounded their trumpet to warn others of danger nearby.

Plant-eaters

Vegetation such as leaves and twigs would have made up most of Parasaurolophus' meals, which meant it needed to live in forested areas where there were lots of plants.

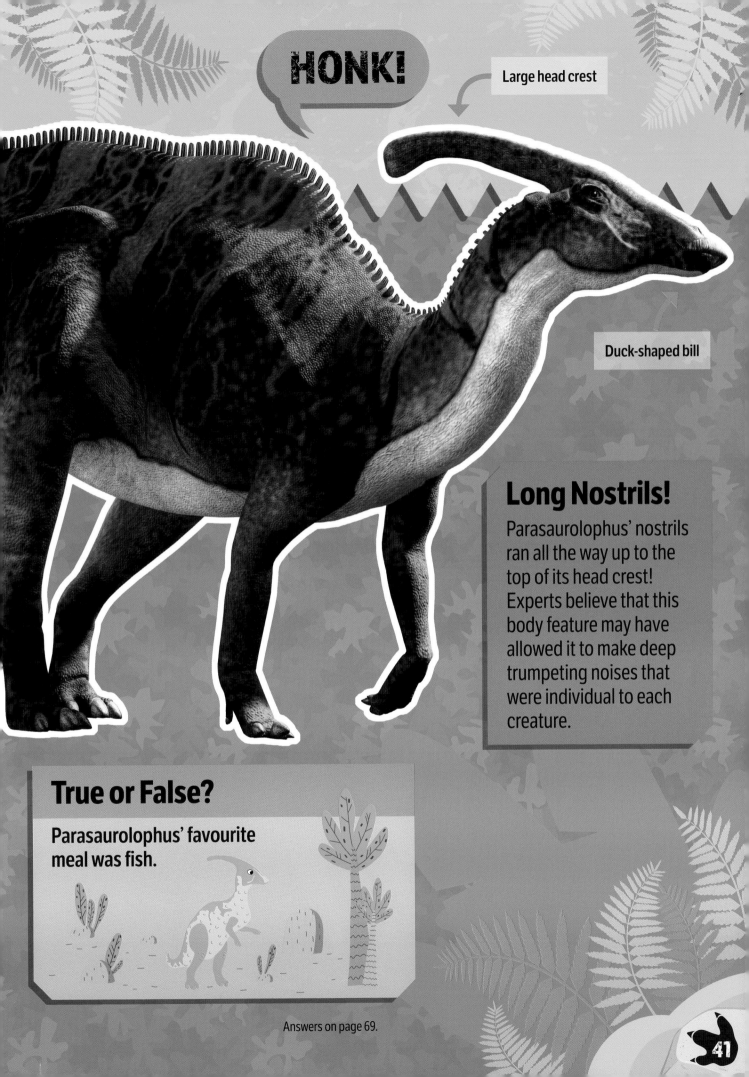

HONK!

Large head crest

Duck-shaped bill

Long Nostrils!

Parasaurolophus' nostrils ran all the way up to the top of its head crest! Experts believe that this body feature may have allowed it to make deep trumpeting noises that were individual to each creature.

True or False?

Parasaurolophus' favourite meal was fish.

Answers on page 69.

CRETACEOUS CARD CRAFT

Make a dinotastic card to send to someone special.

You will need:

- A4 Coloured and white card
- Glue
- Scissors
- Pencils and Pens

Ask an adult to help ⚠️

Carefully follow the steps below.
Remember to ask an adult to help with cutting.

Step 1: Take a piece of card and fold it in half, making sure the white side is facing up.
With the folded edge nearest you carefully draw around your hand, then draw a neck and head outline as shown in the picture below.

Step 2: Cut out both shapes, taking care to leave the fold intact on the hand shape. Refold the card to show the coloured side.

Step 3: Cut out small circles from a contrasting colour piece of card, and glue them to your dino. Open the card and glue the neck and head shape to the inside as shown below.

Step 4: Cut out small circles of white card for eyes, glue to the card and use a pen to finish the eyes and draw a smile on your dino!

Step 5: Finally, write a message inside for someone special.

CORYTHOSAURUS

This helmet-crested, duck-billed dinosaur lived in herds.

Hollow crest

Hollow Crest

Corythosaurus was a large, gentle plant-eater with a hollow head crest that it used to make loud, booming calls to other members of its herd. It may have made these noises as it travelled to keep its group together – or if it came under threat.

It's All in the Name!

When Corythosaurus was discovered, scientists named it after a group of ancient Greeks called the Corinthians. They chose this name because the Corinthians wore helmets shaped similarly to the dinosaur's head crest!

DINO FACTS

Name: *Corythosaurus*

Meaning: *"Helmet lizard"*

Size comparison:

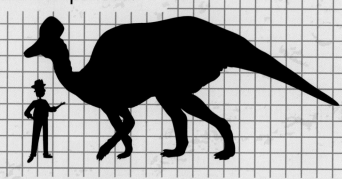

Food: *Plants*

Danger rating: *2/10*

Habitat: *Forests and plains*

BOOM!

BOOM!

Flat, blade-like tail

Two or Four

Like Parasaurolophus, Corythosaurus belonged to the hadrosaur dinosaur group. It could probably choose between walking on all four of its legs or just its back two – and it grew to an impressive 9m (30ft) in length.

All Mixed Up Can you find the missing jigsaw piece to complete Corythosaurus?

A

B

C

Answers on page 69.

COLOUR BY NUMBERS

This duck-billed dinosaur needs colouring in!
Use the colour key to help you complete this dinosaur picture.

JOIN THE DOTS

Join the dots to finish this plant-eating dinosaur, then colour it in!

PARASAUROLOPHUS

PREDATOR vs PREY

Some dinosaurs were expert hunters, while others were peaceful plant-eaters!

Mighty T. rex

Possibly the most well-known dinosaur of all time, T. rex was a fearsome predator — and probably a scavenger, too! Its body was perfectly suited for hunting, with banana-sized teeth to bite into prey and a super powerful jaw to hold it in place. No wonder its name means "king of the tyrant lizards!"

What Did it Eat?

Flesh! T. rex would have hunted other dinosaurs that lived at the same time, such as the duck-billed dinosaurs. Recent evidence suggests that T. rex could have also hunted in packs, like wolves. Scary!

Growth Spurt

For a long time, experts thought there might have been a second, smaller species of T. rex, but it is now believed that they simply took their time to grow, doubling in size during their teenage years!

TYRANNOSAURUS REX

Under Attack

There is firm fossil evidence to indicate that T. rex hunted the plant-eater Edmontosaurus. Its fossilised bones show signs of T. rex bite marks and even healed wounds! Edmontosaurus lived in large herds that travelled thousands of miles — perhaps T. rex followed and picked off the weaker dinosaurs?

Veggie Diet

Unlike T. rex, Edmontosaurus didn't spend its time searching for animals to eat. Instead, it grazed on plants such as conifers. This large duck-billed dinosaur had a wide, toothless beak and hundreds of cheek teeth that it used to grind up plant matter — even tree bark!

Protecting Itself

Edmontosaurus didn't have many body features for self-defence, but it did have thick, tough skin. Experts believe that it was able to move at fast speeds to dodge potential predators, too.

EDMONTOSAURUS

GIGANOTOSAURUS

Known for its sheer size, this huge dinosaur roamed prehistoric South America.

Southern Lizard

The mighty meat-eating Giganotosaurus roamed what is now Argentina in South America during the Cretaceous period. It feasted on large plant-eaters and had no natural predators of its own.

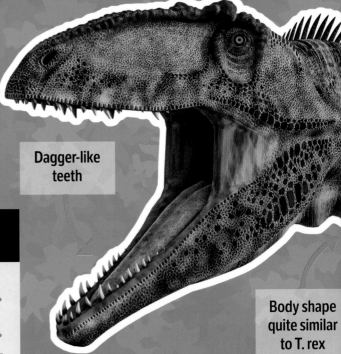

Huge head but small brain

Dagger-like teeth

Body shape quite similar to T. rex

DINO FACTS

Name: *Giganotosaurus*

Meaning: *"Giant southern lizard"*

Size comparison:

Food: *Meat*

Danger rating: *9/10*

Habitat: *Forests*

Big Head

Imagine a dinosaur with a head even taller than you! That's Giganotosaurus! This massive dinosaur measured around 13m (42ft) long and is thought to have been quick on its feet, reaching speeds of 48 km/h (30mph)!

Search the Word

How many 3-letter words can you find in

GIGANOTOSAURUS?

Glossary box:

An animal that is hunted by another animal (a predator) is called prey.

Powerful legs

STOMP!

STOMP!

Hungry Hunter

Giganotosaurus probably scavenged for food as well as seizing any opportunity to attack its prey. Its super sharp teeth were perfect for slicing and wounding the animals it hunted.

Fierce Theropod

Giganotosaurus belonged to the theropod dinosaur family, which ranged in size from tiny to very large. Even though some looked very different, all theropods were carnivores, had bird-like feet and typically walked upright.

DINOSAUR DISCOVERY

Find all of the different dinosaurs, then colour them in.
How many of each did you find? Write your answers in the boxes!

ARCHELON

The largest turtle to have ever lived!

DINO FACTS

Name: *Archelon*

Meaning: *"Mighty First Turtle"*

Size comparison:

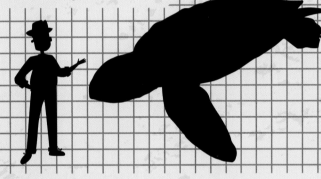

Food: *Squid, fish and sea plants*

Danger rating: *0/10*

Habitat: *Open ocean*

SPLISH!

SPLASH!

The Size of a Car

The Archelon, is not a dinosaur, but an extinct ancient relative of today's turtle. It grew to an incredible 4.6m (15 ft) long and lived towards the end of the Cretaceous period alongside the dinosaurs. It is thought to have looked similar to the leatherback turtles in our oceans today!

Soft Shell

Unlike today's turtles, Archelon couldn't withdraw its head or flippers inside its shell for protection. It also had a much softer shell than the turtles alive today. It is possible that if its shell had been hard, it would have been too heavy to swim!

Thin shell

Broad front flippers

Laying Eggs

It is thought that Archelon left the sea to lay its eggs on sandy beaches, like modern turtles. It probably spent the rest of its time cruising the ocean surface for food or avoiding predators – such as sharks.

How Many?

Count all the **Archelon** eggs on the page.

There are ☐ *eggs!*

Answers on page 69.

CODE BREAKER

See if you can crack this cool code to work out
the answer to the question below.

A	B	C	D	E	F	G	H	I	J	K	L	N
26	25	24	23	22	21	20	19	18	17	16	15	14

M	O	P	Q	R	S	T	U	V	W	X	Y	Z
13	12	11	10	9	8	7	6	5	4	3	2	1

What do many scientists believe caused the extinction of the dinosaurs?

26	8	7	22	9	12	18	23

An _____ hitting Earth.

56

FOSSILISED FOOTPRINTS

Follow the footprints to find the wandering dinosaur
that left them behind!

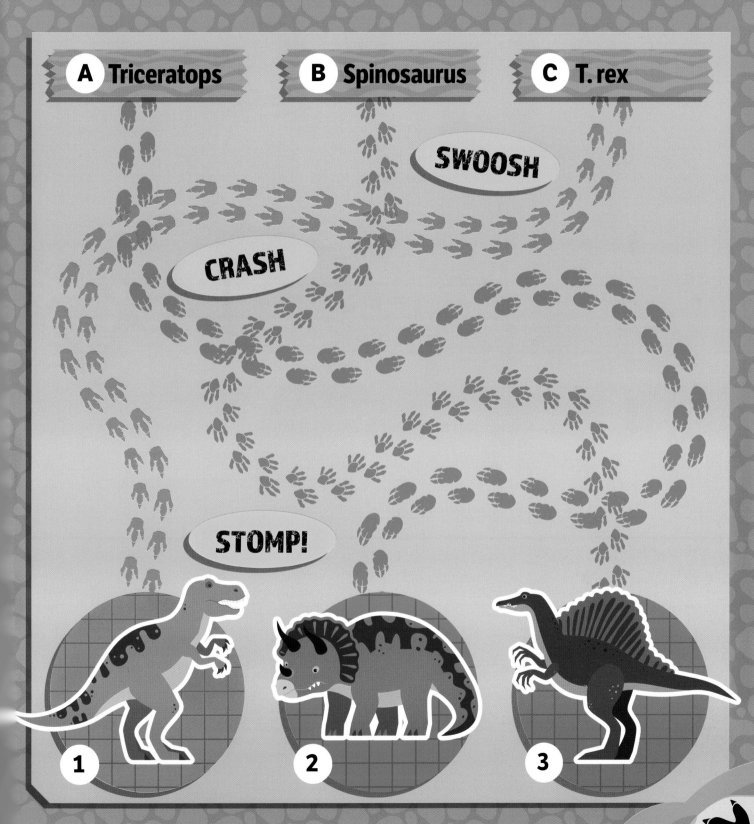

A Triceratops   **B** Spinosaurus   **C** T. rex

SWOOSH

CRASH

STOMP!

1

2

3

TODAY'S DINOSAURS

Did you know that the birds we see today are descended from dinosaurs? It's true!

Feathery Friends

Birds such as chickens, pigeons and even ostriches all evolved from theropods – the meat-eating dinosaur family that included T. rex. Fossil remains show that the earliest birds, such as Archaeopteryx, looked far more like dinosaurs than today's birds.

Bird Evolution

Since they emerged, birds have evolved in thousands of different ways to suit a variety of different habitats. Most have flight, others live on the ground — and some can swim! Importantly, they have managed to survive by adapting to Earth's many changes.

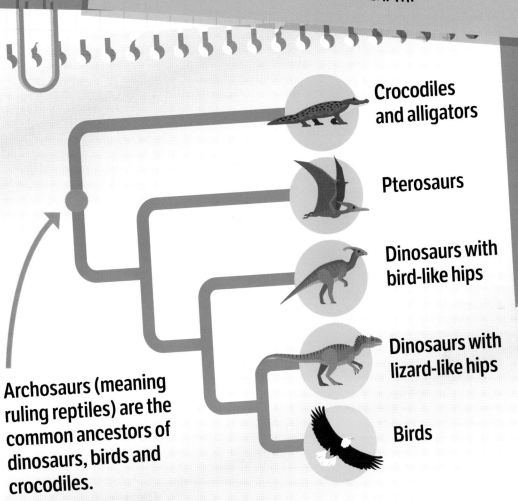

Crocodiles and alligators

Pterosaurs

Dinosaurs with bird-like hips

Dinosaurs with lizard-like hips

Birds

Archosaurs (meaning ruling reptiles) are the common ancestors of dinosaurs, birds and crocodiles.

Are Crocodiles Dinosaurs?
Like dinosaurs, crocodiles and alligators are reptiles that evolved many millions of years ago.
These ancient-looking creatures certainly look like they are related to dinosaurs, but they are, in fact, not related as closely as you might think — even though they do share a common ancestor (relative).

TROODON
The smart, feathered dinosaur.

Big eyes and well-developed eyesight

Feathered Dino

Troodon was a small, smart dinosaur that lived during the Cretaceous period. It had lightweight bones, a feathery body and ate meat (such as mammals and lizards) and plants. Its large eyes show us that it may have also been nocturnal.

Sharp, serrated teeth

SCREECH!

DINO FACTS

Name: *Troodon*

Meaning: *"Wounding Tooth"*

Size comparison:

Food: *Meat and plants*

Danger rating: *5/10*

Habitat: *Woodlands*

Super Smart Dino

It is possible that Troodon was the smartest dinosaur of all time. That's quite a title! Scientists have worked this out by looking at its brain size in relation to its overall size. Compared to other dinosaurs, it comes up trumps!

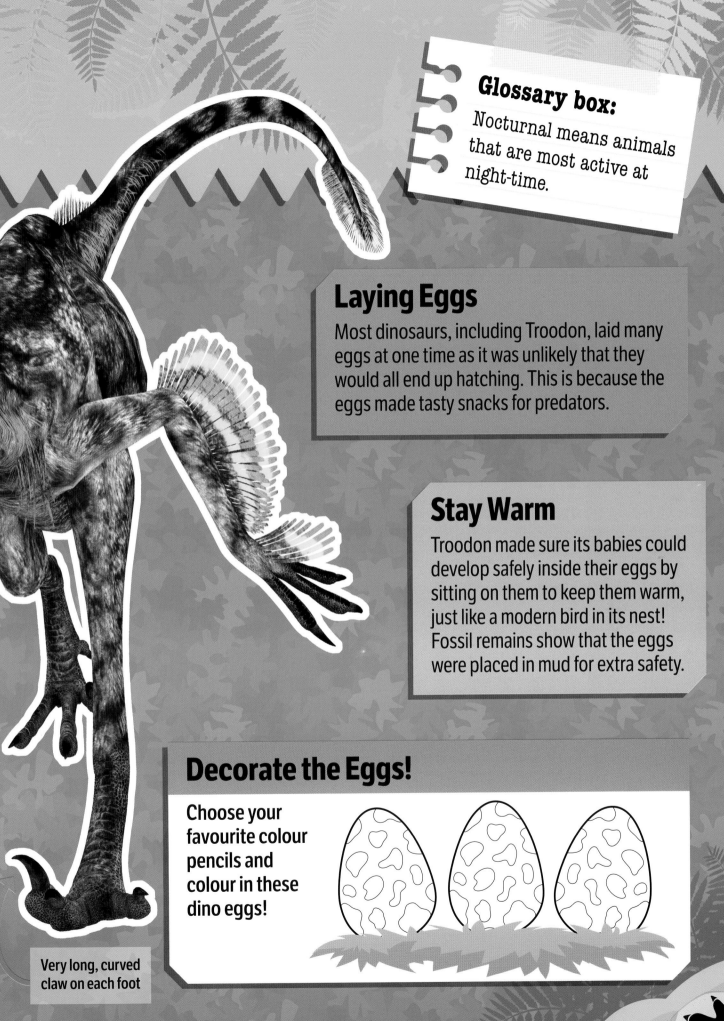

Glossary box:
Nocturnal means animals that are most active at night-time.

Laying Eggs

Most dinosaurs, including Troodon, laid many eggs at one time as it was unlikely that they would all end up hatching. This is because the eggs made tasty snacks for predators.

Stay Warm

Troodon made sure its babies could develop safely inside their eggs by sitting on them to keep them warm, just like a modern bird in its nest! Fossil remains show that the eggs were placed in mud for extra safety.

Decorate the Eggs!

Choose your favourite colour pencils and colour in these dino eggs!

Very long, curved claw on each foot

WORD SEARCH

There are 10 dino words hidden in the grid below, can you find them all? Tick the correct box each time you spot one!

C	L	A	W	S	R	G	C	R	B	C	H	N	L
A	S	T	E	R	O	I	D	Z	U	R	Y	T	W
U	J	H	R	C	W	P	C	H	O	E	P	B	I
M	U	M	A	I	G	Z	O	L	X	T	G	C	H
Y	R	M	H	D	A	A	D	T	V	A	I	J	Y
Z	A	G	T	I	R	S	P	P	V	C	W	P	G
S	S	T	M	B	I	O	S	M	O	E	I	G	E
A	S	I	C	X	K	B	S	I	Z	O	V	D	O
U	I	W	J	I	S	H	B	A	C	U	Z	X	L
R	C	P	D	F	H	P	T	D	U	S	P	U	O
O	F	E	H	P	S	P	B	U	W	R	Q	I	G
P	D	T	H	E	R	A	P	O	D	J	D	W	I
O	I	Z	C	A	K	G	X	X	I	S	K	F	S
D	E	X	T	I	N	C	T	I	O	N	X	Y	T

- [ ] **CRETACEOUS**
- [ ] **HADROSAUR**
- [ ] **EXTINCTION**
- [ ] **TRIASSIC**
- [ ] **GEOLOGIST**
- [ ] **JURASSIC**
- [ ] **CLAWS**
- [ ] **ASTEROID**
- [ ] **SAUROPOD**
- [ ] **THERAPOD**

Answers on page 69.

CROSSWORD

Use your dino knowledge to solve the clues and fill in the crossword below.

Hint!
Letters are shared when the words cross over each other.

ACROSS

3. When a species has completely died out

6. An animal that eats plants

7. A scientist that studies the history of Earth

8. An animal that is hunted by other animals for food

DOWN

1. An animal that eats both plants and meat

2. An animal that eats meat

4. An animal that hunts other animals for food

5. Preserved remains of a plant or animal in rock

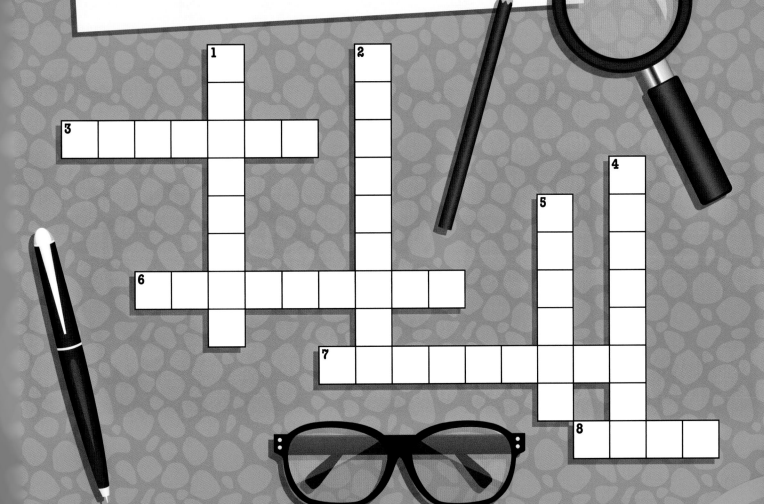

Answers on page 69.

COELOPHYSIS

This early dinosaur was small but speedy.

Built for Speed

Coelophysis was a small theropod dinosaur that lived towards the end of the Triassic period. Its body structure was specially adapted for speed, helping it to hunt for small reptiles and insects.

DINO FACTS

Name: *Coelophysis*

Meaning: *"Hollow form"*

Size comparison:

Food: *Meat, including insects and reptiles*

Danger rating: *1/10*

Habitat: *River floodplains*

Small body

Light, hollow bones

RIP!

SNARL!

Teeth and Claws

To hold onto the animals it caught, Coelophysis had sharp, saw-like teeth and gripping claws. It needed these special body features as it didn't have size on its side – it only grew to around 2m (6 ½ft) in length.

Hunting in Packs

There is plenty of fossil evidence to suggest that this early dinosaur lived in groups, which means that they may have hunted larger prey together in packs, a bit like wolves do today.

Long tail gave balance

Weighed less than 30kg (66lb)

Unscramble the Word

Hint: What dinosaur group did Coelophysis belong to?

THREOOPD

Answers on page 69.

WHO AM I ?

Read the clues and study the dinosaurs.
Can you work out who they are?

1 I had a bill like a duck and a fancy head crest.

2 I was a giant meat-eating dinosaur.

3 I was a small dino, with lots of sharp teeth.

4 I was a huge, long-necked dinosaur.

Tip:
If you need help remembering the names of the dinos, don't forget to look through the pages of this book!

5 I had a huge sail on my back.

6 I had a beautiful neck frill and three horns on my face.

Answers on page 69.

TRUE OR FALSE?

Test your memory by answering the questions!

Circle the correct answer!

1	The dinosaurs died out 120 million years ago	True	False
2	Archelon is a type of plant-eating dinosaur	True	False
3	Spinosaurus probably ate fish	True	False
4	Triceratops' favourite meal was meat	True	False
5	Birds are living descendants of dinosaurs	True	False
6	Dinosaurs belong to the mammal animal family	True	False
7	Pteranodon could fly	True	False
8	Corythosaurus had a super thick forehead	True	False
9	Giganotosaurus weighed 500 kg	True	False
10	Coelophysis hunted in packs	True	False
11	T. rex belonged to the theropod dinosaur group	True	False

ANSWERS

p.11 SIMPLE DINO-DOKU

p.12-13 MAZE CHALLENGE

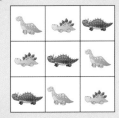

p.15 TRACE THE TRAIL! Trail B

p.16-17 DINOSAUR DISCOVERY

2　6　7　3　4　1　5　8

p.21 WHICH COMES NEXT? D, C, E, B, A

p.26-27 SPOT THE DIFFERENCE

p.31 SPOT THE DINO! Picture **2** is a Pteranodon

p.35 ODD ONE OUT Dinosaur **2** is the odd one out.

p.36–37 ONLY JOKING!
Q.1 = F. A Dino-snore!
Q.2 = H. Tea, Rex?
Q.3 = E. Rep-tiles!
Q.4 = D. Tricera-cops!
Q.5 = B. It was too rocky!
Q.6 = G. An Edmonto-chorus!
Q.7 = C. A dino-sour!
Q.8 = A. A really 'saur-loser!

p.41 True or False? - False – Parasaurolophus ate plants

p.45 All Mixed Up - Piece A

p.52–53 DINOSAUR DISCOVERY

p.55 ARCHELON
There are 6 eggs.

p.56 CODE BREAKER ASTEROID

p.57 FOSSILISED FOOTPRINTS
A. Triceratops = **2**
B. Spinosaurus = **3**
C. T. rex = **1**

p.62 WORD SEARCH

C	L	A	W	S	R	G	C	R	B	C	H	N	L
A	S	T	E	R	O	I	D	Z	U	R	Y	T	W
U	J	H	R	C	W	P	C	H	O	E	P	B	I
M	U	M	A	I	G	Z	O	L	X	T	G	C	H
Y	R	M	H	D	A	A	D	T	V	A	I	J	Y
Z	A	G	T	I	R	S	P	V	C	W	P	G	G
S	S	T	M	B	I	O	S	M	O	E	I	G	E
A	S	I	C	X	K	B	S	I	Z	O	V	D	O
U	I	W	J	I	S	H	B	A	C	U	Z	X	L
R	C	P	D	F	H	P	T	D	U	S	P	U	O
O	F	E	H	P	S	P	B	U	W	R	Q	I	G
P	D	T	H	E	R	A	P	O	D	J	D	W	I
O	I	Z	C	A	K	G	X	X	I	S	K	F	S
D	E	X	T	I	N	C	T	I	O	N	X	Y	T

p.63 CROSSWORD
Across
3. extinct
6. herbivore
7. geologist
8. prey

Down
1. omnivore
2. carnivore
4. predator
5. fossil

p.65 UNSCRAMBLE THE WORD THEROPOD

p.66-67 WHO AM I?
1. Corythosaurus **2.** Giganotosaurus **3.** Coelophysis
4. Apatosaurus **5.** Spinosaurus **6.** Triceratops

p.68 TRUE OR FALSE?
1. False – it was 66 million years ago
2. False – it was a giant turtle
3. True
4. False – it was a plant-eater
5. True
6. False – they are reptiles
7. True
8. False – it was Pachycephalosaurus
9. True
10. True
11. True